TWINZILLA

Also by Barbara G. S. Hagerty

The Guest House (2009), chapbook
Motherfish (2012), chapbook

twinzilla

POEMS BY

BARBARA G. S. HAGERTY

HILARY THAM CAPITAL COLLECTION

2014 Selections by Jeanne Larsen

THE WORD WORKS

WASHINGTON, D.C.

The Word Works, PO Box 42164, Washington, DC 20015
wordworksbooks.org editor@wordworks.org

Cover art: Richard Hagerty, "Twinzilla," 2013, oil.
Author photograph: Richard Hagerty
Book design: Susan Pearce Design
Library of Congress Control Number: 2013916633
International Standard Book Number: 978-0-915380-90-9

Gratitude to publications in which poems have appeared, some in earlier versions:

Motherfish (Finishing Line Press, 2012): "Twinzilla Two-Faced,"
    "Omnikleptophilia," "Bella Donna," "Recruit,"
    "Spring Break," "Motherfish," "Mother."
Jasper: "The Kids Don't Know Everything."
The Guest House (Finishing Line Press, 2009): "Child," "Lump."
Sow's Ear Poetry Review: "Twinzilla Paleontology."
Qarrtsiluni: "Twinzilla Incommunicado" (first published as
    "Father at Night").

ACKNOWLEDGMENTS

Special appreciation to Jeanne Larsen, poet and director of the Jackson Center for Creative Writing at Hollins University, for selecting *Twinzilla*; warmest thanks to Nancy White and Karren Alenier of The Word Works for the uncommon energy, passion, and skill they have brought not only to the publication of this work but also to many others; and to the Poetry Society of South Carolina for nominating my manuscript and to Susan Meyers and Debbie Scott for their roles in bringing about this opportunity. And to Susan Pearce for her inspired design work.

And to the South Carolina Arts Commission for my Fellowship in Poetry (2010-2012), during which time many of these poems were written, as well as to poet/judge Alan Shapiro; also to the sponsors of *The Porter Fleming Poetry Contest* and to Molly Brodak (for selecting "Lizard," 2nd place winner, 2011).

Finally, heartfelt thanks to the many friends and colleagues—poets, novelists, and non-fiction writers—who have contributed in ways tangible and intangible, material and spiritual: Virginia Beach, Peter Benjamison, Libby Bernadin, Tom Blagden, Helen Brandenburg, Henk Brandt, Erik Calonius, Carol Ann Davis, Nathalie Dupree, Dottie Benton Frank, Susan Harrigan, Mary Harris, Ann Herlong-Bodman, Sheridan Hough, Kurt Lamkin, Alice Levkoff, Kit Loney, Mary Alice Monroe, April Ossmann, Debbie Scott, Anne Rivers Siddons, Gary Smith, Susan Finch Stevens, South Carolina Poet Laureate Marjory Wentworth, Katherine Williams, and Joe Zealberg. To Tippy Brickman, Sandi Mohlmann, Carolyn Rivers, and Teri Tyree, for friendship and enthusiasm. My deepest thanks to surrealist poet Richard Garcia and lyricist Susan Meyers who, while perhaps opposites on the poetry spectrum, converge at the point of excellence as writers and teachers extraordinaire.

ACKNOWLEDGMENTS

For Gervais, Curry, Hart, Andre, Anthony, and two Richards

Contents

I.

II.

III

Double, double, toil and trouble...

—Shakespeare, *Macbeth*

I find I incorporate gneiss and coal and long-threaded
moss and fruits and grains and esculent roots,
And am stucco'd with quadrupeds and birds all over...

...

To be in any form, what is that?

—Walt Whitman, *Song of Myself*

1.

Like Life

It probably isn't human nature to feel someone
is building a simulacrum of you, slightly
out of reach, like the SubZero hums 24/7
churning out frozen rectangular copies.
Why not aspire to transparency?
Don't be fooled by what you think you think.
Somewhere along the line, I had a falling out
with fallout—id iddn't what you think. Ergo, ego.
Oh, damn this superannuated nonce, this cold spot—
what light differentiates genii and congenital,
and what maternal genetrix? I may as well
marry my doorbell. O, spitting, untrustworthy image,
you are my dead ringer.

Twinzilla Disambiguation

Homuncula, you ape me perfectly
in your outward mimicry. A knock-out
knock off, complete with shiny hoodtop finial.
But underneath, in the engine,
who but we can map that *terra incognita*?
Cartographers imagined monsters of the deep,
arms waving like Shivas into the gaping
unknown. Down deep,
I've long known your faithlessness,
your disconnect. Don't get the impression
I'm not fooled by wave and wavelength.
Even after we leave the grid, it will still
be bump and grind, touch and go.
My clone, my souped-up waxwork. Do you copy?

Beetle

This day has birdsong in it,
and a color like regret, wishful,

half-imagined, the beginnings of a woolen scarf
on abandoned needles. Your death

hasn't been recorded yet,
the book of hours open to a page

of three hummingbirds sipping nectar
at the day's long proboscis,

a sapphire beetle in the magnolia bloom
I broke off yesterday and placed in a vase,

emerging from his fragrant white rooms
into our ordinary bewilderments,

the page riffling this way and that,
in a light, directionless wind.

Child

Repeatedly I dreamed
myself armless
as a carved chess piece.

All night, an unseen hand
moved me
from square to opposing square.

Mornings, I walked to school
exhausted, doing my best
to impersonate a normal child.

All day, my body
stiffened with splinters
from the bark of a disfigured tree.

Twinzilla Flip

Although you wear my disguise as if you owned it,
every viewpoint has a flip side,
every mirror mirrors true reverses.
Siam are you, and so am I, in this shared cashmere twinset,
you borrowing clothes which do not the woman make,
rummaging in my psyche's closet night and day,
trying on my poems, jamming your iambs in my shoes.
If the shoe fits after the FAQs are answered,
let Drake's Equation pass like a far night train
freighting our dreams toward a distant sunny palm.
The palm at the end of the mind, like Wallace S. said,
imagining the relentless binaries would be SWAK,
knowing the heart's envelope could be further pushed.

Bella Donna

Beautiful lady, my mother said,
but I wasn't fooled.
Behold the small girl
in the waiting room, her dilated eyes,
spooked by her walk
down the doctor's gangplank,
letters wiggling like minnows
in shadowy shoals...
Which is clearer?
Lenses flipping,
Z floating to an archipelago
of albino islands
in the doctor's legerdemain...

                    No wonder
I sought a first-row seat,
became a scholar
of blackboard and chalk,
lover of color, spy, thief,
catechist of dust motes,
pupil of the dark-eyed dark,
infatuate of close-ups, nightshade, belled speech,
consort of dandelions,
swami of paper clips
and fingers' ten crescent moons,
expert at buttons and low-flying insects.

Twinzilla Fortune

Although objects in mirror *are* closer than they appear,
do not tamper with evidence that the world spins
in wormhole time and may not be receding
backwards down a two-lane blacktop laundry chute.
While clouds wring out their lingerie,
tune your yoyo to cosmic microwaves,
brace yourself for the bad-girl sideways rodeo,
followed by cheap chow mein and chopsticks
and crackling pronouncements by paper oracles.
Consider you may be your very own astral projection
or a chew toy in the nursery of gigantic gods who dwell
in parallel universes. Meanwhile, appearance does count,
so try dry cleaning to remove those damn spots.
Inspect your chassis on an annual basis for signs of age—
next, why not buy supersized? What've you got to lose?
YOU COME INTO MONEY. YOU HAVE HAPPY LIFE.

Last Afternoon of a Centenarian

I drove through geologic time,
asphalt displacing salt marsh,
oaks, youngish, rooting in magma.

Winter had surprised the forsythia.
Few sparrows were about.
A whirlybird spun atop the Cloister's roof.

Inside, immortal silk orchids collected dust.
Closets held unnecessary suitcases.
Dressed, seated in a Queen Anne chair,

you praised the newest Lincoln biography,
emancipation's thrilling history.
You inhaled a little slipstream of oxygen;

I drank a glass of water.
The satin-lined hour
held secret compartments.

I suspended my disbelief.
You had something up your sleeve:
a coin thrummed over your shoulder,

a rabbit, the knave of hearts.
The trickster afternoon sawed itself in halves.
Now I see you, now I don't.

ABCDs

Listening to ABBA play on CD,
I deconstruct existential Legos.
If I am, by any other name, a rose,
then metaphysics are like candy
and linguistics ought to be expendable
like tonsils, Kleenex, pantyhose,
paper, plastic, or last year's clothes,
for who'd confuse a *bonbon* with eternity?
Spare me bombast, euphemism, doubletalk.
I prefer the clarity of pointed spears,
storm petrels, shaken pears, and pet rocks.
Gimme shelter from wordy helter skelter.
Let's put the *nature* back in nomenclature.
Time to take Doggerel for a walk.

Motherfish

It was the summer of translations,
forcing nouns into undershirts,
knotting bibs around verbs.

On the coping,
lizards changed clothes,
ghostwrote their memoirs.

Under the umbrella's
penumbra, I'd become
a very old child.

Mother breathed through gills,
swam golden loopholes
in the pool.

Her feet were footnotes
on my gloss.
She swam in cursive.

Clouds coined new clouds.
Fleet phrases
flew off the water's shoulders.

Such hydraulics, freight
and displacement of text,
heavy lifting.

Flesh into ether,
her body's strokes.
She wrote in invisible ink.

She made it look easy,
Motherfish,
the deep, the rope, the ladder.

Twinzilla Cautions

Do not accept packages from unknown persons.
Beware non-native strangers who may be concealing
hazardous contraband "down there."
Question algebra. Dismantle thoughts traveling
the brain's baggage carousel in parabolas.
Do not conflate equations or make them up.
Ask yourself if you are in it for the long haul.
Distrust creation myths, theories of falling,
masks, opportunists, undercooked meat.
Consider whether St. Francis's path crossed Rumi's.
Compute the sum of your Apgar, SAT, IQ scores,
and divide by your age to determine your lucky number.
Some say there are no lucky numbers
but *to check or carry-on, that is the question.*
Others say there's one big final and it's Pass/Fail.
Report any suspicious activity to the nearest agent.

Remote

I predicted
my slide toward thickness,
long tooth, short memory,

but what about scales
of justice, of slippery fish,
shorted-out wiring,

the peering up
over glasses
at the indecipherable gizmo

floundering in my hand?
Clouds of dusky moths
accompany my pony-and-cart,

my old school, old hat, wind-up clock,
through days' long slouch,
post-meridian, past glass dioramas

of stuffed primates and plastic shrubs,
the quaint array of eight-tracks,
typewriter, land line, rabbit ears,

the black-and-white TV set
as I haul and haul them on my back
toward the far horizon.

The Kids Don't Know Everything

Like rice on white, you are my default setting,
lug-nut, pocketknife, knight-in-shining-anorak,
my *no chance of showers*, my hole card, my *who knew?*
To our kids, we're so *yesterday*, so *over it*,
so, you know, *analog*. Let's give them a break,
deal them in. My Freudian slip's pink,
your holds no-barred. There's no place
like down and dirty, the old folks' ghetto,
so don't put off what you can do yesterday.
I mean, the buck stops. The cow cashes.
Dreamboat, I say, blood's not thicker
than a pair of snake eyes. My lottery ticket,
best guess, rain check, tool kit, flyswatter.
I drank the Kool-Aid. Kids, you do the math.

Between them one *r*, that's how close

I coexist with friend and fiend.
Whole continents shift in my tectonic plates.
The ocean's implied in this glass of water.
Awaiting the report, and hearing, at last,
on the phone: *your path is clear.*
Is the doctor speaking in koans?
Then orchestras of crickets explode in the pond,
tiny cosmoses overflow, the body goes on.
I stuff the world in my mouth:
the fritillaries, blood oranges, all the garish sunsets.

Slow Work

An old man begins
the slow work of dying,
removes his hearing aids,
naps through morning.

He doesn't speak
of abandoning his loved furrows
and secret places, silver fur
at back of the neck,
skin's heat, a sliver of cuticle.

He doesn't mention
the body's disobedience.
His glasses rest at his side,
the newspaper has fallen
in sheaves onto the floor.

He doesn't ask,
How many more times
to touch an ear,
brush a crumb away,
push back a strand of hair?

Sometimes it seems
he has already left the animal
who'll not leave, who's still
devoted to its master.

Twinzilla Disturbology

Even before you majored in disturbology,
we were already *dui generis*. Though all talk
is theory, the moment's warehouse stores
swizzle sticks, quantum mechanics, Larry Levis's
Great Aunt No One. Tune an ear to the turning universe,
its valves' whoosh and fall. Doesn't everybody have
an "evil twin" who sings inside the wreck?
O, doublemint and paradox, my once lush and easy-speak,
when White Russians downed Pink Ladies in Margaritaville
and Manhattan, when we lived on Planet Ashtray.
When you were my armed and dangerous,
sound and fury, crash and burn, we shared a skin.
I'm still here with my rack and pinion, lock and load,
my alive and kicking, my warm and fuzzy.
Here, put on my robe and bunny slippers. Sleep deep.

2.

Twinzilla Incommunicado

I can't tell you anything with words.
It's not that you can't hear.

You listen as a stone listens to rain,
as the sea's murmur fills the tympanum,

as this bromeliad's cupped leaves
capture their thimble of rain.

A daughter's work has come to this,
bringing a bread loaf to the bedside,

a bunch of wild goldenrod cut from a ditch.
Night comes and reveals the moon,

silent in its black factory,
stamping flower and weed, indifferently.

Archaeology

Decades later, the scenery remains the same.
Yellow jasmine fences the palms
like crime scene tape, druids
from a herstory no one's bothered to write.
So much in plain sight overlooked:
the crape myrtle's pink curlers unfurling
next to the pool's pump house,
clouds genetically linked
to the cumulous fifties,
the globed, openface tomato sandwiches
disintegrating on a platter like ruined civilizations.
Why shouldn't the soul's wilderness
be plotted exactly here, alongside
every buried gerbil, every girl's
starched, pressed pinafore?
The August air's freighted with hairspray,
dividends. Beyond the garden's brick perimeter,
an elderly driver has set off the alarm again
in his new-fangled car, shrieking the afternoon
into layers that can't be excavated,
not properly, not in any way you could trust.

Late Bronze

Elegant, draped
on the *chaise longue*,
she wore the expression of a sphinx.

When I put drops in her eyes,
she opened them, her look
one of exaggerated wonder.

The week reticulated,
and time hid in tesseracts
while her gown grew tendrils.

She reclined long hours
beside a bowl of cooling soup,
a ziggurat of saltines.

She grew elongated,
chilly and classical,
a version of someone's mother

unfolding in silent cascade
and being revealed,
line by continuous line.

Grounded

His arm's gone slack, a wing with a claw,
invisible pins pricking his heart.

A wilderness of blackness presses
on the window, a slow dawn waiting

for the milkman's bottles,
glass notes trumpeting dim light.

Morning is a membrane, a hat, a sock.
When did his mother retreat

into an old black-and-white photograph,
who left his golf clubs out in the rain?

His daughter drives him to the doctor,
who can find nothing wrong, except oldness.

He is mired in oldness, the body's effrontery,
dappled in brown spots, as though

he created his own shade, camouflaged
from even himself, the agile man

who vanished, leaving this birdcage of flesh,
two plastic hearing aids in a chipped saucer.

Twinzilla Disequilibrium

In a deadzone between *Help* and *Information*,
the dial tone drones *Om*, accusing me
of *attentional rubbernecking*. Pardon me
if my myth-making machinery's closed for repair,
making mitochondria and skinned knees my go-to.
After a few false starts, most of us finally get in touch
with the Big Crunch, the Little Bang. With the right
utensils, you can smoke out any liar, fry any trainwreck.
Sentient beings on the fast track do not epiphanies make,
and hordes just want to score the best stadium seats.
For the rest of us, any forgery naturally feels real.

Twinzilla Solipsism

Somewhere between fractals and waves,
I came across my former self, dead Barbara,
in need of a permanent no longer.
The oldtimers discussed the *Lawd Jesus!* days
when we could fix mishaps with our Allen wrench.
We were night-foundered, hitting speed bumps
on the William Tell highway,
falling apples braining us like fallacies.
Some days were mashups, some were the usual
snafus and red tape, but we imagined
a future of heuristics and buckyballs,
graphite, and diamonds—and so it broke,
a rumble and stampede of icy asteroids,
an inversion of forensics as the cosmic trapdoor opened
and I myself became something to disprove.

Channeling Hokusai

From asanas, I hang like a bat
over the flax mat,
ride confetti surf,
scroll and fold
to origami.

From pigeon, crane,
views cycle by:
clouds' cows and plows,
and slivered trees.

From corpse pose,
one pine bough is a forest;
from lotus,
a plump green muscle;
from cobra,
a pair of lacquered chopsticks.

Mother

Forceful, I say,
where you'd say *mild* or *soft*.
Molded, soldered, bulleted, spent.
Staked eight legs
on four strong stalks
with hair, brains, eyes, energy.
Potential. Useful, I say,
and don't underestimate
my body's camera,
its zoom lens and light shutter,
crucible, kiln,
humid bellows,
and capable oven,
its photosynthesis.
I was entered and exited,
I exuded and extruded,
earth moved through me,
film, magma, flesh.
Genius, I call
my dirt petticoats,
and beautifully rent:
stamen and husk,
petal and root.

The Blossoms Unknown to Linnaeus

In the hours Mother tunneled,
her arms were filthy scrolls
I committed to memory,
her hands torn vellum,
veins striated igneous rootlets.
I hung on monkey bars
while she recited
the four patterns in nature:
spiral branch meander explosion—
Glancing backwards,
she hacked with her spade,
trenched, scraped, tamped.
She called the withered bodies
of frogs *children's souls*,
and when a robin flew
in retrograde through the house,
she buried our silverware in the yard.
Her iced tea sweating as she dug,
she wore a ripped peignoir
and read the leaves between
the lines of dirt and dissolution,
incubated seeds under her tongue,
tasting the same-old-same-old's music,
fastening shiny fish hooks onto stems,
tiny mirrors, sequins, sewing needles,
her trowel hand raw, filling
with earth's black stigmata.
I was her nettle, thorn and balm,
her yellow jackets and sperm,
her countenance and stone.
Obbligato.

Prelude to an Elegy

I want to build
you a poem with a fuselage
of feathers and ibis bones,
fly you out of here,

but the railed bed's rigged
and swallows you up,

it's a racing sloop
whose sails swell with morphine
as the room swoons.

Warrior in a cotton nightgown,
you ride in and out of consciousness.

Too young to understand,
your little boy's at home.

On the bedside table,
capsized objects
flaunt their permanence:
hairbrush, silver mirror,

a vase of red zinnias
that will outlive you.

Twinzilla Grist

Some grateful bastard says God controlled
the bullet's path, another claims randomness.
Thoreau found strong evidence: a trout floating in milk
belly-up in its microuniverse amid wet reflections
of moons, rings, and other elliptical matters.
Even the Milky Way evades classification,
is neither curdled cheese nor chocolate.
So what if the whole Vatican vacations in the Poconos,
and I need to take out a second mortgage on my disbeliefs?
What comes around is no joking matter for comedians,
and what's kosher may just be grist for your candy bar,
so many laps around the rumor mill. It's just me again,
aliasing as you, Twinzilla—so, go, go configure.

Empty Nest

En passant meant: I lost another pawn.
Bad Bishop: I was cornered. I castled
in the rookery, nursery, garden, laundry,

and when I looked up twenty years later,
the cow bird had feathered my nest with imposters.
Quills in the Maytag spurred me to espionage,

to pace the linoleum's vacant checkerboard,
divining the tumbled careless blossoms
forgotten in pockets—buttercups (ingratitude),

hortensia (you are cold), rue (disdain)—and flocks:
wilderness of dirty t-shirts, malapertness
of pajamas, murmuration of children's socks.

Twinzilla Two-Faced

What is the world if not gnomic, gestural?
Long ago, my first lesson—tell the truth
yet conceal its essence. Like a spoon
in a glass of water, clear but bent,
or cowlick hair, or walleyed iris,
the facts would misrepresent the ditzy
player, tied of tongue, so skilled at cards,
scrambled words, and memory tasks,
she was barred from birthday party games.
To the disassembling ark came, two by two,
yin-yang, black-white, pepper-salt, lovers-friends.
Close I hold my hand—and yours.

Ode to Ugly Words

Let's hear it for *zit, yucca, worm, wienerschnitzel, vermin,*
vomit, turd, turgid, subpoena, snot, smegma, and *snark*;
throw a parade for *rural, quahog, pustule, pus, pulchritude,*
puce, ointment, nacre, mutton, mucus, mung, and *jizz*;
put *ignoramus, legume, kumquat, gout, fistula, fug* on *Oprah*!
No more second-class citizenship for *flatulence, flaccid,*
exhume, dude, chigger, carbuncle, buttocks, bratwurst;
make stars of *bubonic, besmirch, albumin, anus*;
liberate Quasimodos, Calibans, Uriahs
from the dismal swamp of the off-stage gulag. Let all pariahs
spread wings over the free world of lingual archipelagos,
find, if not love, then equal billing with other queens
of the gorgeous diaspora—*mellifluous, susurrus, murmur*—
the Misses Swimsuit, Congeniality, and redhot runners-up;
put rhinestone crowns on *dandruff, pissant, fructify, scrotum, yuck.*

Twinzilla Fine Print

Avoid the royal *we*.
Read the fine print on the window's wire mesh:
this screen will not prevent anyone,
or anything, from falling out.
Try cilantro instead of rebar.
Recall that our formulae, like centers,
do not hold, but disintegrate like burned-out red giants
plunging in free-fall through the galaxy.
If the shoe fits, hurl it through the window.
If it breaks the window, make a new shoe
from glass—or light shattered on terrazzo.
Don't conflate jaw and jewel,
yawn and yarn, fib and rib.
Remember a suitcase is neither milk nor turbine,
that love, given time, enacts
a periscope, dogtrot, on-ramp.
Of all geometries, feathery is best.
Meteorologists forecast a plague of ringtones.
When all else fails, chew one hundred times.
Grip the wheel at ten and two o'clock.

Impermanence

Some days I'm content
to read the Upanishads

understanding my journeywork
is like a meteor's

and other days I take an apple
from the cut-glass bowl

with a pang for a future
without its round heft

in my palm
the smooth membrane

of its circumference
its scent of appleness

like no other
the red curve

concealing glossy black seeds
in the core

the dimpled absence
at the top

where the brown stem
once held fast to the tree

Ravenous

What I want today isn't everything,
merely all of one thing—

the magnolia's creamy lip
undulating like a snowfield

no human has traversed,
its litter of pink-tipped anthers

like piled matchsticks, or one hummingbird's
heartbeat feathering in my hand.

The moment of release—what is that?
To be sprung, tension on a latch released,

or swept free—white tablecloth's
disencumbrance of crumbs?

Sun ransacks the day, a thief
overturning what's hidden,

emptying the day's pockets
with practiced finesse.

Recruit

The powerful forearm.
The stainless steel watch.
The buzz cut
and dog tags.
The olive-green t-shirt.
The huge
tight-laced desert boots
bracketing a backpack.
The soft tissue
and spinal cord: whole.
Four limbs: intact.
Bootstraps and wishbones,
clean shave, ammo, camo, duffel.
Tenderfoot, sharpshooter,
grenadier, samurai, rookie
at the airport
waiting to board.

Sea Island Tomatoes

Hard rain unsettles the ground,
stirs damp storehouses of snails
and chipped teacups, the leaves' ears
dissolving into summer's progression
of explosions, cannas, mosquitoes,
the evening's cathode rays
in whose violet lights an old man
wraps himself in a July blanket, a woman
calls a child into supper, a summons
sounding across decades.
It's not too late, though the hours
are tremulous and so much unspoken,
to unspool the days, to return
the broken dinner plate
to the raised hand, which then lowers
to set minor moons spinning
in a girl's braids on a winter morning.

The yard dims to thin porcelain
as shadows brush the windows
and lights turn off in the world's libraries.
The night surrounding this house
is a vast book doomed to go unread,
like a lost civilization in a far latitude,
a strangler fig's millipede feet devouring
the last syllable spoken, last crude utensil.
The father sits at the window, the blue glare
of news buffering him from the day's capacities
which drift over the river to the green fields,
ripening coiled yellow buds into tomatoes,
here and now, for the taking.

Spring Break

Thinking his song private, inaudible,
a boy home from college sings

as he casts at the pond for red drum.
Downwind, winter makes its closing

arguments: last leaves
let go of the scrub oaks,

invisible nurseries open
their closets of pollens and spores.

It's March, warm. Milk wells
in new dandelion stems, clouds subdivide

commodious mansions of fish.
As wind lifts his solo,

the scales merge into pure flight
and nothing, nothing to speak of.

Slug

i.
A punch, landed square—
breath-taking smack—
an eighteen-wheeler
running the light.

ii.
Subway token, counterfeit coin
fed to the mouth
of a casino slot or turnstile.
Fortune: entry granted—
or denied.

iii.
Rotgut, backyard-brewed
or bought cheap from a red dot store,
decanted, cupped,
or swigged straight up—
knocked back and knocking back.

iv.
After the deluge,
the beery baptism:
spineless, creepy gourmands
of garden lettuces
float capsized in an amber pond.

v.
Flattened on the sofa
in word pastures
of books and newspapers:
a splayed-out body, inert, pillowed,
all day Sunday, supine.

Twinzilla Arm Wrestling

Even after the good twin wrestled the evil sister
into something like submission, fungi still flourished
in hidden places, and stars burned at a furious rate.
Changing fuses in my funky basement, I understood
Chaos was no mere Theory, *mon semblable*.
Even mannequins try on masks, and each sister
wants *her* foot to fit the glass slipper.
We dress up, play house, horse-play,
our changing of the guard in the *Who's Who*
of the personality's pantheon of goddesses.
Whoa, you croak, but I say Diane Arbus knew
freaks hanging out on ordinary divans draped
with protective plastic ate the same Coney Island
hotdogs as suburbanites daytripping at the beach.
No amount of hairspray can disguise you or convince me
you are not the bombshell and the bomb.

3.

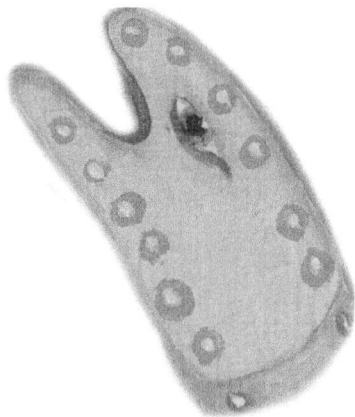

M

On the morning I woke up as the letter M,
my body parts refused to answer to their usual handles.
An overhead thought bubble announced *matters*
of nomenclature should be yielded to foofing dogs
or gardeners wielding leaf blowers.
I went at an egg-wife-trot to my Skinner box of words
all serving a life sentence for non-compliance.
Quidnunc, quoth the maven, *whatever floats your boat.*
Handwash personal items and do not attempt this at home.
M's not bad, deep cleavage, *murmury*, *mum*, and *mammary*,
as meanwhile my mouth, medulla, muscles, and middle finger
hummed and *mmmm'd* to *mellishorn*, *mallserback*, and *minshush*.
I won't turn up the hole card, get saved on the river.
Easier to straighten out the Messier Objects.
O, poem dismembered, O, disobedient footsoldiers.

Twinzilla Compartmentalization

He is still here.
Neither allegorical nor extinct.
Older than old.

If his head cracked open,
it would split
into Humpty-Dumpty
city-states: Time, Color,
Memory, Forgetfulness—

that he excelled in.
He still patrols
those impassable borders.
Daddy Warships,
Father Rustysides.

Lump

The bad coin no woman wants,
deplorable marble. I, red-handed,
caught you—my ticket to
the gulag: one way or not?

Benign, be my Valentine.
I wait nine days to be benign.
Benign becomes a prayer
rolled over the tongue,
like hard candy I suck and suck
to draw sweetness in.

Lump. Like stump. Like clump.
Like stub and stubble. Unreal. The body
makes its own bad deals.
Doesn't consult me.

Be my Cloud Nine, benign,
my new favorite word,
let me pluck you from *The Merck Manual*,
and make you mine.

Lump in my throat,
in my oatmeal. Lump,
I have no affection for you,
only for all of me that isn't you.

Benign, I learn, is mine,
to roll upon my tongue's
every sensor:
salty, bitter, sour, sweet—
I take it in and in.

Twinzilla Newsflash

Newsflash from planet Baa-Baa-Black-Sheep:
arthritic Labradors occupy every kitchen,
perfecting tricky omelettes in watched pots.
Meanwhile, surreptitious astrophysicists
pull foolscaps over the hospital corners
of the sleeping multiverse. Should I explain
my love is not a Wiki entry or a wind-up toy?
Not under warranty or battery-operated?
Entrenched as I am in the karmic footlocker,
after eons of meting out this or that,
and now this lame banging and MAJUSCULES for emphasis...
yet something golden glitters at the glottal subway stop.
Hail Barbara full of *excrementus taurus*,
whose coupons may or may not be redeemed
in the bigbox store of life. Woman up!
You whose mouth fills with entreaties:
O, shelf life! O, bone spur! O, plantar fasciitis!

Lizard

This is how you live when you have no other choice:
splayed on a rock in full sun, ruby throat pulsing,
gliding up a stalk to watch, changing shades,

slipping into a green robe, unable to glance away,
or turn, ever, to stone. Sometimes I see them approaching

over the grass, the parapet, in the street, and a part of me
naturally wants to turn away, to lock the safes of my heart,
but I can feel a tremor like the first moment

a tuning fork is struck, and so the swelling tones
become irrefutable, sunlight having its way

on a day of storms or uncertainties, branches
bending their capacities to the vagaries of wind.

Twinzilla: Caveat Emptor

Under penalty of law enforcing dustballs,
lost action figures, last year's popcorn,
and a guerrilla splinter faction,
do not remove tag from this mattress.
A *deus* AWOL from the *machina* may hang out
unseen in the ticking with El Niño affects,
bedbugs, stubborn stains, bad dreams, dust mites.
Beware the blow dryer's sirocco,
the vacuum cleaner's vortex, lest it suck up
lost earrings, love notes, good intentions, PIN numbers.
Do not drop your plugged-in appliance in water—
prevent electrocution of innocent mallards in bathtubs.
Guard your identity as you would your power strip.
Do not pick up anything that's smoldering or on fire.
O small gods, sealed in blister-packs!
Worlds turn on smaller axes than Costco monuments.
Read the fine print. Get your beauty rest.
Use only as directed. Trust me on that.

Bad Karma Day

Today my enormous shadow
projects a very small person.

I'd rather be an ungulate
picking my sure way up the red cliffs
outside town, indifferent
to other ungulates,

interested only in the next mouthful
of clover at the next elevation,
not these admonishments recirculating
like tainted water in a rusty pipe,

not these people who got up
on the wrong side of the bed.
Numerals drop off mailboxes;
the postman wanders the streets,

unable to deliver anything.
Everyone has a bad dream
to recount in excruciating detail,
but there are no more listeners.

The landfill overflows
with terrible deeds,
and nothing decomposes.

Night Inventory

                              A doll house
comes to mind: small plastic father,
a blue suit lacquered on rigid limbs,
faux brick fireplace, painted coals.

                         Don't ask me
what happened on the moon's far side,
or what became of the tiny, battered clocks,
plaid sofa, frying pan, hooked rug.

                         What I know is
somewhere in a town lost
as a board game forgotten in an attic,
a girl tends an artificial hearth,
a woman hangs her apron on a diminutive hook.

                              Tonight
is a cardboard roof,
and under it, a daughter doll
still waits in a rocking chair.
Milk floods the house.

I want it back.

Quantum Twinzilla

In case of fire, break glass and take a leap.
Recall all borders are fluid and permeable,
all walls host to wolf and rabbit silhouettes.
Look for hand signals, celestial portents.
Here's the church, the steeple, a pew of paper dolls.
An infinity of you in receding mirrors.
Believe in dark matter, black holes, and also
in the un-Disney, who colorizes
the black-and-white film waltzing
in your head. Yield to any excuse
for consort or consortium. Use #3 pencils.
Jump the broom, gun, to conclusions.
Disregard the Dewey Decimal System.
Remember the world's gone digital
though our hands long for analog,
for holding. A cozy burning log
to chase away the existential chill.
Leap over the spectrum of everything you know.
Dress for crazy weather. All is collage, to be continued.

Omnikleptophilia

Sunlight taught its lessons in larceny early on
as I rehearsed declensions in school-girl Latin,
all gall, all gall, all gall, all gall, all gall.

Polishing my penny loafers in the cloak room,
amo amas amat. Conjugating by moonlight,
pickpocketing taxonomies, lifting coinage.

Between episodes of backstabbing and Nabs,
Hannibal's elephants grazed Alpine meadows;
Caesar had his way, *vini, vidi, vici.*

The puellae grew apart and vanished like sfumato
into purloined obsessions. No protocol exists
for my chosen form of thievery, and I'm guilty

of taking love from unguarded sources:
the waiter dressed like Jung, asking *cooked or raw?*—
the bee drunk on the dregs of limoncello.

Twinzilla Dither

Like the grunge band in the basement,
the undulations came as a surprise.
While Heimlich maneuvered a beefsteak
and Schrödinger's cat napped,
lipid panelists were I.M.-ing, as usual.
Although the opposite of irony may be wrinkly,
the moment you're born, you're air, milk, shit, history,
and since history permits all things, I personally
carbon date myself from *before* the Big Bang.
My pacemaker may be your gold pocketwatch,
but my reality show is not your comeuppance,
so ask if I want chickenfeed or backscratchers.
I'll specify *one if by zither, two if by pianoforte.*
Sooner than apocalypse, it all comes to bricolage.
Dear Twinzilla, why not sit under sodium vapor lights
and rename constellations: Golden Arches,
Midnight Kangaroo, i-Pad Charger, Armani's Belt?
Your long distance annunciation is my short-order cook,
the fortune in my cookie the warning on your safety matches.
Toothpicks prop up our lightweight identities.
Soon: the meat hook, shove-off, dirt goodbye.

Impending Absence

I'm already schooled in it:
the dent in your chair back
where leather memorized you.
Your scent, in sweaters and hats.

You were always absent:
not like keys or a favorite
umbrella gone missing,
but in the way a boulder
on the far mountain
acknowledges no one,
the way a current finds its way
around all impediments.

So I am well prepared
for the geography you inhabit
to be usurped by bees, who do
what they must do continuously—
without sentiment, without instruction.

Twinzilla Paleontology

We squandered days, we ran amok, our humor was dark,
but the night sky never failed to lower its chandeliers.
We traveled light and pitched our tent in a blind spot between hoax
and promise, we understood the possibility of lucid dreaming.
All messenger pigeons were grounded, tropes surrounding me
like old suitcases, the labeled cells and diaried hookups,
oracular telephones, surely goodness and mercy, etc.,
a primitive campfire burning at mind's remotest edge.
Flocks of Darwin's finches. A hat brim full of candles.
We were somewhere between Bodhisattvas and recycling,
on a day of successive approximations and coming
closer, but to what, I couldn't say. But closer.
Still, we were understudies to minnows, we drank
cold water, we tore bread apart with our hands and ate.

Early Mourning

A grey bird nests in your tinfoil hair.
A scarecrow has stolen your wardrobe.
Your limbs clatter like coat hangers.

Hold still, and I'll climb on your forehead's cliff.
Say anything, and I'll cast myself on your breath-wind.
Recline, and I'll acrobat around you.
Be patient, and I'll build you cradle and tomb.

I stare at the boats of your feet and declare myself a mariner.
But when I set you loose, I find I'm tethered.

Postcard Mailed from the Future

A room without mirrors, a room without you,
but I'm getting ahead of the likely story,
mailing postcards to the dead-letters office:
Recipient moved, address unknown. Night scales
vertical walls, furniture cairns, sheets twisted
like drifts of improbable snow, unmated socks,
the shed nightgown. On the flip side of canceled
stamp and scribbled hand is the pictured land—
head, heart, hinter, border, no man's—
our old familiar fertile valleys, voluptuous
slopes, ivory faces of moon and clock,
the frayed, flayed mattress latitudes—
picnic crumbs, sex, newborns, unfinished books.

Twinzilla Wormhole

While all things are permitted in carbon fluctuations,
who knew the keeper of the Zoo Hypothesis
would permit one dark horse to escape through a clause
in the Alpha Quadrant? Meanwhile, David Quammen
writes *homo sapiens* is the biggest weed of all.
Overhead ghostcams record far-out games
in parallel meadows where a futurehood of shepherds
rolls the knucklebones of sheep over past pastures.
So what my bandwidth is not much longer than a song
on FM, and I see strictly in ROY G. BIV.
Leave it to fruit flies to expose
The Law of Falling Bodies fallacy, let their vertigo
be my lug wrench, my haft, my hive, my lucky queen.
I am bankrolled by unseen forces.
I'm all bluffs and burn cards, sorting
through Dark Matter, Light Matter, No Matter,
the scattered dice of stars, the hitchhiking tumbleweeds.

The darkness sends instructions

for translating the millefleur language of bees
into stalactite torches inflaming damp grottos,

for constellating your longing's scarlet grandiflora
with transits of swan, fish, and lyre.
In the machinations of peristalsis, you do not differ

from an anole or whelk, and like the water buffalo and Lucy,
you metabolize oxygen into carbon knives
aimed at the spinning heavens, transubstantiate

whole catalogues of seeds and filaments.
Even the dirt is a thesaurus best read with bare hands.
You've already been selected down the generations

into Darwin's gorgeous taxonomies, mysterious
as the warm cave of your own mouth, and which serves you
even at your most unthinking and ungrateful.

Native Daughter

Of austerities, the sky
over this garden is ignorant.

Swallows chase the day
like Isadora.

If I am too much here,
my claim's a native one.

Six Meyer lemons bloom
in their terra cotta condos.

The fountain repeats itself
to the revolution of hours.

Prosperous novelists and minor
movie stars occupy pastel mansions,

whose lots touch my leafy perimeters.
Winter's a rumor over Minneapolis.

Pleine aire artists angle easels
to paint the enviable precincts.

On satellite maps, my house
mimics a lucky playing card.

Clouds loll about like drunk tycoons,
the harbor swirls with buttercup yachts:

The Branch Office, Runaway, Okra Soup,
Segue, Mom's Mink, Caper, Bliss.

74

Naming the Girl

after Rhett Iseman Trull

Call her *Firestar. Titania* or *Palace.*
Not Susan, Nancy, Debbie, or Barbara....
Can't you just see *Cosmica* in her space suit,
lassoing quasars, first to travel

at the speed of light? Give her a name
to defy all gravities: *She-Ra, Neytiri.*
One to define gravity, like *Crescent.*
Luna, Oberon. Make her other-worldly, *Phanta,*

or so worldly her name embodies it: *Terra.*
Let her be a divining rod for pleasure, *Alice Wonder,*
Sappho, Jewel-Above-Price. Incendieria
will invent a new way to make fire:

thumb against palm igniting skin.
Call her *Acetylene—Torch* for short, or *Scorch.*
Give her an axis-turning, Atom-Eve smashing
name to demolish borders:

Macha, Hercula, Iconoclasta,
galloping up the birth narrows,
past Rigel, Betelgeuse, Alpha Centauri,
vernix-slick, sinuous, strong. Get it right the first time:

Ishtar. Nectar. Blossom-Breaking-Into-Light.

Twinzilla Fandango

Grubworm, switchback, lightbulb, Venus flytrap:
a bright idea has you by the ovaries
just when your mare goes missing on the astral plane.
The usual effluvia about overhead bins, emergency
exits, while cognoscenti relive their birth trauma,
spray graffiti in aerosol on your brain's moving sidewalk.
What do you want anyway, Bodhisattvas?
Extraterrestrials, the reinstatement of Pluto?
Hone your skill set for the coming days,
partake of hook-ups, reruns, second helpings.
Will you nurse the same old wounds in the new multiverse?
Lock your tray in the upright position. Wheels up!

ABOUT THE AUTHOR

Barbara G.S. Hagerty is a native of Charleston, South Carolina, whose poetry publications include *The Guest House* and *Motherfish*, both chapbooks from Finishing Line Press. Awarded the 2010-12 Fellowship in Poetry from the South Carolina Arts Commission, she is a member of the Long Table Poets, a workshop led by Richard Garcia. She also co-coordinates the Piccolo Spoleto Sundown Reading Series, held early each summer in Charleston, and is a board member of The Poetry Society of South Carolina. She has worked as a photographer, curator, journalist, essayist, and teacher of poetry and creative non-fiction, and has published several non-fiction books. She holds an MA in Creative Writing from The Johns Hopkins University Writing Seminars.

ABOUT THE ARTIST

Richard Hagerty is an American surrealist painter. He cites among his influences the imagery and iconography of eastern and western religions, mythology, dreams, philosophy, nature, and astronomy. Widely collected and exhibited, he has been the focus of numerous one-man shows and is represented by The Corrigan Gallery (corrigangallery.com) in Charleston. His work may also be seen at www.richardhagertyart.com.

ABOUT THE WORD WORKS

The Word Works, a nonprofit literary organization, publishes contemporary poetry and presents public programs.

The Hilary Tham Capital Collection presents work by poets who volunteer for literary nonprofit organizations. Nominations are due from qualifying 501(c)3 non profits by April 1, manuscript submissions by May 1. Other imprints include International Editions, the Washington Prize (book publication and a monetary award for an American or Canadian poet), and, starting in 2014, The Tenth Gate.

Monthly, The Word Works offers free literary programs in the Chevy Chase, MD, Café Muse series, and each summer, it holds free poetry programs in Washington, DC's Rock Creek Park. Annually in June, two high school students debut in the Joaquin Miller Poetry Series as winners of the Jacklyn Potter Young Poets Competition. Since 1974, Word Works programs have included: "In the Shadow of the Capitol," a symposium and archival project on the African American intellectual community in segregated Washington, DC; the Gunston Arts Center Poetry Series (featuring Ai, Carolyn Forché, and Stanley Kunitz); the Poet Editor panel discussions at The Writer's Center (including John Hollander, Maurice English, Anthony Hecht, Josephine Jacobsen); and Master Class workshops (with Agha Shahid Ali, Thomas Lux, Marilyn Nelson).

As a 501(c)3 organization, The Word Works has received awards from the National Endowment for the Arts, the National Endowment for the Humanities, the DC Commission on the Arts & Humanities, the Witter Bynner Foundation, Poets & Writers, The Writer's Center, Bell Atlantic, the David G. Taft Foundation, and others, including many generous private patrons. The Word Works has established an archive of artistic and administrative materials in the Washington Writing archive housed in the George Washington University Gelman Library. The Word Works is a member of the Council of Literary Magazines and Presses and distributed by Small Press Distribution.

More information at WordWorksBooks.org.

TO OUR SUPPORTERS

We wish to thank the generous donors whose contributions to the Hilary Tham Capital Collection made this year's books possible. In addition to some who asked to remain anonymous, we also extend gratitude to Karren Alenier, Nathalie Anderson, James Beall, Sandra Beasley, Mel Belin, Doris Brody, W. Perry Epes, Barbara Goldberg, Joseph Goldberg, Stephen Hubbard, Tod Ibrahim, Brandon Johnson, Steven Klimah, Richard Lyons, Kathleen McCoy, Susan Laughter Meyers, Miles Moore, Debra Ragan, James Ragan, John E. Ragan, J. Courtney Reid, Brad Richard, Maritza Rivera, Hannah M. Stevens, Barbara Louise Ungar, Maria van Beuren, Mike White, Nancy White, Rosemary Winslow, Pamela Murray Winters, Michele Wolf, and Dallas Woodburn.

FROM THE HILARY THAM CAPITAL COLLECTION

Mel Belin, *Flesh That Was Chrysalis*

Doris Brody, *Judging the Distance*

Sarah Browning, *Whiskey in the Garden of Eden*

Grace Cavalieri, *Pinecrest Rest Home*

Christopher Conlon, *Gilbert and Garbo in Love*
  Mary Falls: Requiem for Mrs. Surratt

Donna Denizé, *Broken like Job*

W. Perry Epes, *Nothing Happened*

Bernadette Geyer, *The Scabbard of Her Throat*

James Hopkins, *Eight Pale Women*

Brandon Johnson, *Love's Skin*

Marilyn McCabe, *Perpetual Motion*

Judith McCombs, *The Habit of Fire*

Miles David Moore, *The Bears of Paris* & *Rollercoaster*

Kathi Morrison-Taylor, *By the Nest*

Tera Vale Ragan, *Reading the Ground*

Maria Terrone, *The Bodies We Were Loaned*

Hilary Tham, *Bad Names for Women* & *Counting*

Barbara Louise Ungar, *Charlotte Brontë, You Ruined My Life*

Jonathan Vaile, *Blue Cowboy*

Rosemary Winslow, *Green Bodies*

Michele Wolf, *Immersion*

WASHINGTON PRIZE BOOKS

Nathalie F. Anderson, *Following Fred Astaire*, 1998

Michael Atkinson, *One Hundred Children Waiting for a Train*, 2001

Molly Bashaw, *The Whole Field Still Moving Inside It*, 2013

Carrie Bennett, *biography of water*, 2004

Peter Blair, *Last Heat*, 1999

John Bradley, *Love-in-Idleness: The Poetry of Roberto Singarello*, 1995,
    2ND edition as e-book, 2014

Richard Carr, *Ace*, 2008

B.K. Fischer, *St. Rage's Vault*, 2012

Ann Rae Jonas, *A Diamond Is Hard But Not Tough*, 1997

Frannie Lindsay, *Mayweed*, 2009

Richard Lyons, *Fleur Carnivore*, 2005

Fred Marchant, *Tipping Point*, 1993, 2ND edition 2013

Ron Mohring, *Survivable World*, 2003

Brad Richard, *Motion Studies*, 2010

Jay Rogoff, *The Cutoff*, 1994

Prartho Sereno, *Call from Paris*, 2007

Enid Shomer, *Stalking the Florida Panther*, 1987, 2ND printing 1993

John Surowiecki, *The Hat City after Men Stopped Wearing Hats*, 2006

Miles Waggener, *Phoenix Suites*, 2002

Mike White, *How to Make a Bird with Two Hands*, 2011

Nancy White, *Sun, Moon, Salt*, 1992, 2ND edition 2010

INTERNATIONAL EDITIONS

Yoko Danno & James C. Hopkins, *The Blue Door*

Moshe Dor, Barbara Goldberg, Giora Leshem, eds.,
    The Stones Remember

Moshe Dor (Barbara Goldberg, trans.), *Scorched by the Sun*

Lee Sang (Myong-Hee Kim, trans.), *Crow's Eye View:
    The Infamy of Lee Sang, Korean Poet*

Vladimir Levchev (Henry Taylor, trans.), *Black Book of the
    Endangered Species*

ADDITIONAL TITLES

Karren L. Alenier, *Wandering on the Outside*

Karren L. Alenier, Hilary Tham, Miles David Moore, eds.,
  Winners: A Retrospective of the Washington Prize

Christopher Bursk, ed., *Cool Fire*

Barbara Goldberg, *Berta Broadfoot and Pepin the Short*

Jacklyn Potter, Dwaine Rieves, Gary Stein, eds.,
  Cabin Fever: Poets at Joaquin Miller's Cabin

Robert Sargent, *Aspects of a Southern Story & A Woman From Memphis*

CPSIA information can be obtained at www.ICGtesting.com
Printed in the USA
LVOW04s0033180814

399537LV00002B/30/P